UNDERWATER HAWAI'I

Exploring the Reef

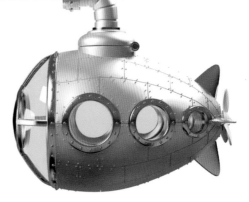

ULYSSES BOOKS
FOR YOUNG READERS

Published by:
Ulysses Books for Young Readers,
an imprint of Ulysses Press
PO Box 3440
Berkeley, CA 94703
www.ulyssespress.com

ISBN: 978-1-64604-664-5

Design and text by Keith Riegert
Edited by Renee Rutledge

Printed in Indonesia
2 4 6 8 10 9 7 5 3 1

Images from Shutterstock.com unless otherwise indicated
Cover: © Shane Myers Photography (front) and © Ocean Image Photography (back, pages 4, 28); *Interior:* porthole © Andrey_Kuzmin; page 1 © Melissa Brandes; pages 1, 3 © ilterriorm; pages 3, 21 © Shane Myers Photography; page 4 © Ernst Heinrich Haeckel (small image); page 5 © Darren J. Bradley; page 6 © Jesus Cobaleda; page 7 © Molly NZ; page 8 © chonlasub woravichan; page 9 © Andrea Izzotti; pages 10, 13 © Peter Douglas Clark; page 11 © Beat J Korner; page 12 © Marty Wakat and © COZ (small image); page 14 © KITTIPONG SOMKLANG; page 15 © Pavlo Burdyak; page 16 © RobJ808 and © Arunee Rodloy (small photo); page 17 © Kristina Vackova; page 18 © Henner Damke; page 19 © Jessica Heim; page 20 © Tabooma; page 22 © Longjourneys; page 23 ©MCKaske; page 24 © RobJ808; page 25 © Arunee Rodloy; page 26 © gary powell; page 27 © Brandon B and © O.Bellini (small image); page 29 © Greg Amptman; page 30 © Pawe? Borówka; page 31 © RugliG; page 32 © Daniel Huebner; page 33 © _lego 19861111; page 34 © NFKenyon; page 35 © Silent O; page 36 © lawoel (left), © TeddyandMia (middle), © RugliG (right), and map courtesy of the Library of Congress, Geography and Map Division.

This product conforms to all applicable CPSC and CPSIA standards. *Source of production:* PT Macananjaya Cemerlang in Central Java, Indonesia; *Date of production:* February 2024; *Production run:* PTM202402-1

Welcome to Hawai'i! Before you put on your snorkeling mask and dive into the warm Pacific Ocean, let's learn about some of the amazing sea creatures swimming about the islands' coral reefs. Did you know that, since Hawai'i is so far away from any other landform, about one in every five fish in the shallow reefs can be found *only* in Hawai'i? Beneath the surface of the ocean, you will spy everything from colorful butterflyfish and long, skinny trumpetfish to majestic green sea turtles and even shy reef sharks. Let's take a look!

Marine invertebrates

The Coral Reef

All the fish that you read about in this book make their home in Hawai'i's coral reefs. It may look like rock, but coral is actually more of a living city made up of hundreds of thousands of tiny marine invertebrates together in a colony.

Humuhumunukunukuāpuaʻa

The reef triggerfish is the state fish of Hawaiʻi. When hunting, the reef triggerfish shoots jets of water to uncover tasty food in the sand. It can also change colors and makes a snorting sound when it's scared!

Redlip Parrotfish (uhu palukaluka)

A fish that poops sand? Yup! This fish feeds on algae-covered rocks using its hard mouth that looks like a parrot's beak. Whatever parts of the rock it can't digest come out as sand. (The beach is just A LOT of fish poop.)

Forceps Butterflyfish
(lau-wiliwili-nukunuku-'oi'oi)

Like many other butterflyfish, the yellow longnose butterflyfish has a fake, dark "eye" on its back fin to trick larger fish about where it's swimming.

Unicorn Tang (kala)

This fish's horn isn't the only cool thing about it—the unicorn tang also has sharp blades on its fins to fight off bigger, meaner fish. If you see this fish in the water, be careful. . . it's sharp!

Trumpetfish (nunu)

These long, skinny, and brightly colored fish are closely related to sea horses. They are sneaky hunters that quietly inch up to their prey without being noticed.

Ornate Butterflyfish

Like the forceps butterflyfish, the ornate butterflyfish is one of approximately 129 different species of butterflyfish. This little fish is shy and hides in the coral, where its striped body helps it blend into the reef.

Hawaiian Cleaner Wrasse

The cleaner wrasse is the ocean's version of a car wash. These fish set up a "cleaning station" on the reef and then wait for customers. Other fish stop by to have parasites stuck on their bodies eaten off by the wrasse.

YIKES!

Spiny Pufferfish (kōkala)

Also known as porcupinefish or blowfish, these spiky creatures use air to inflate themselves up to three times in size, making them too big (and sharp) to try to eat.

Hawaiian Whitespotted Toby

The mischievous little Hawaiian spotted toby has the bad habit of biting other fish for no reason. If you see fish that have tiny bites taken out of their fins—it likely came too close to a spotted toby!

Moorish Idol (kihikihi)

The Moors of North Africa believed these beautiful reef dwellers brought happiness. Several really long spines at the top of their dorsal fin give the Moorish idols their unique trailing tail that flutters as they swim.

Yellow Tang (lauʻipala)

One of the reef's most colorful fish, the yellow tang has a special superpower for hiding in the coral. At night it changes color, replacing its bright yellow with a boring gray-yellow to hide from predators.

All grown up

Frogfish (Juvenile)

What a weird-looking fish! This baby frogfish sure looks a lot more like a frog than a fish. But if you think it looks strange now, check out what it looks like when it grows up!

Devil's Scorpionfish (nohu ʻomakaha)

Can you find the scorpionfish in this picture? A master of camouflage, this poisonous fish hangs out on the bottom of the reef waiting for small fish to pass by before snatching a little snack.

Dragon Moray Eel (puhi kauila)

Did you know there are 40 different species of moray eel in Hawai'i? The odd-looking dragon moray eel is one of Hawai'i's rarest. What look like horns are actually a second pair of nostrils that the eel uses for hunting.

Whitemouth Moray Eel (puhi 'oni'o)

Moray eels are very important predators on the reef. They like to hide between rocks and coral or in holes in submerged lava. Keep an eye out for the spotted whitemouth moray, one of the most common eels.

Octopus (heʻe)

These *cephalopods* (Greek for "head foot") are some of the most fascinating animals in the ocean. Octopuses can regrow their arms and are very smart creatures—they know how to use tools and solve problems!

Hawksbill Sea Turtle (honu ʻea)

These endangered sea turtles get their name from their pointy, beak-like mouths that they use to snag tasty food, like shrimp, mollusks, and sponges, from between small cracks in the reef.

Spotted Eagle Ray (hihimanu)

In Hawaiian, this ray's name means "magnificent." And it is! Fully grown, the spotted eagle ray can achieve a wingspan of up to nine feet. Often, they are seen in large groups—kind of like an underwater flock!

Whitetip Reef Shark (mano lalakea)

The whitetip reef shark is a mythical guardian in Hawai'i. These shy sharks spend their days lying on the seabed or huddled together in underwater caves (they don't need to move to breathe) before hunting at night.

Slipper Lobster (ula pāpapa)

These colorful arthropods spend their lives (up to 12 years) on the reef and sandy ocean floor, where they are protected by their thick armor and hidden from sight.

Gilded Triggerfish

Did you know the gilded triggerfish has a special protective superpower? It can use its dorsal spine to lock itself in a tiny crevice or hole so no predator can grab it.

Bandit Angelfish

This sneaky fish might look like it would steal your lunch, but it actually likes to eat something almost no other fish (or human) will touch—highly toxic sponges.

Urchin shell without spines

Long-Spined Urchin (wana)

Ouch! Don't get too close to prickly sea urchins; they protect themselves from predators with their long spines (which can grow back if broken!).

Convict Tang (manini)

Common to Hawaiian waters, *manini* are very social and like to travel and forage in large groups. They're quite the sight!

Peacock Grouper (roi)

This large predator is an invasive species in Hawai'i. It doesn't have many predators of its own, in part due to its unique ability to change color and pattern to blend in with its surroundings.

Barracuda (kaku)

With mouths full of razor-sharp teeth, this fearsome fish pack can dart around the reef at 20 miles per hour. Barracuda are naturally curious and like to check out shiny objects.

Red Pencil Urchin (pūnohu)

This vibrant urchin plays a big role in keeping the reef healthy by using its five sharp teeth to eat potentially harmful algae that cling to the reef as it slowly moves along on its tube feet.

Flying Fish (mālolo)

On a boat cruising the islands? You might spot the incredible flying *mālolo*, which escapes predators by jumping out of the water and gliding through the air (sometimes as far as 1,000 feet!).

Hawaiian Squirrelfish ('ala'ihi)

Take a peek under a ledge or crack in the reef—you may find a whole school of these bright-orange fish with big, squirrel-like eyes! Squirrelfish are nocturnal hunters that spend the day snoozing in cozy, safe spots.

Portuguese Man-of-War

Steer clear of this floating creature's painful tentacles and don't mistake it for a jellyfish. It's actually a transparent carnivore, made up of a colony of zooids that travel together on the wind.

Thornback Cowfish

Don't expect this fish to win an underwater race—it's a terrible swimmer that relies on a hard shell and the ability to cover its skin with deadly toxin (ostracitoxin) in order to stay safe.